time&tide

the islands of tuvalu

peter bennetts   tony wheeler

lonely planet

lonely planet publications   melbourne   oakland   london   paris

Time & Tide: The Islands of Tuvalu was several years in the making. It was a collaborative effort, fostered by the government of Tuvalu and produced in Lonely Planet's Melbourne office.

Photographer Peter Bennetts first visited Tuvalu in June 1998. His interest in the country had been sparked after hearing Bikenibeu Paeniu, prime minister of Tuvalu at that time, on a visit to Australia to lobby the Australian Government (unsuccessfully) to change its stance on greenhouse gas emissions in the lead-up to the 1997 Kyoto Earth Summit. This turned out to be the first of many visits during which Peter attempted to capture the essence of life in a country that faces inundation as sea levels rise.

Impressed with the range and quality of Peter's work and recognising that Tuvalu, unlike other Pacific islands, had never before been documented in this way, the Tuvaluan government approached him with the idea of producing a book. Peter's enthusiasm was particularly matched by the late prime minister, Ionatana Ionatana, and the then Secretary to Government, Saufatu Sopoanga, who gained approval from parliament to provide funds to get the book project under way.

Researching the project would have been impossible without the assistance of the government fisheries patrol boat *Te Mataili* in providing transport between the islands. James Conway, an advisor in the Office of the Prime Minister, also provided unerring support and invaluable advice as Tuvalu's representative throughout the project.

By the end of 1999, Peter was in touch with Lonely Planet, but it took another year and several trips to Tuvalu before production began in earnest. Peter then made two further trips in the company of Tony Wheeler, who had developed a keen interest in the Pacific islands and agreed to write the text to accompany Peter's photographs.

Sadly, the Honourable Ionatana Ionatana passed away at the end of 2000 and so was unable to see the project come to fruition. However, he was impressed with an early version of the work and was delighted that, finally, there would soon be a book documenting contemporary life in Tuvalu.

foreword

Tuvaluans are blessed, as divine right or good fortune would have it. This is not mere idle commentary on my part for we are blessed with our customs and culture, tradition and history; we share intense family and island pride; we have the sea, and above all we have our land. Tuvaluans are closely knit through kinship, a small population and a single binding culture. What this mixture stirs up is a sensation that runs deep, a supreme sense of place. All this results in a society that is special, if not unique.

The Pacific Ocean is the largest geographic feature on earth. Yet within the vast Pacific are the tiniest of all inhabited places: coral reef islands and atolls. Tuvalu's nine tiny atolls lie south of the equator and west of the dateline, but only just. On each atoll lives a little-known group of people, of whom I am one.

I was a very junior civil servant in the colonial administration in the 1960s when I was first exposed to the idea of Tuvaluan independence. Outside critics dismissed the idea saying the odds of self-determination succeeding were poor. Tuvaluans held firmly to an opposite view: we felt the odds of success were tempting if not irresistible. What we wanted was the chance to prove that independence was a task our talent and tenacity were equal to. It is one thing to look back on an era, yet quite another to look at how things are today.

Not so long ago, life in Tuvalu was somewhat different. The ready reasoning is that back then life was simpler, which is partly true and partly the cunning of nostalgia. Simple though day-to-day living in Tuvalu might once have been, life then was also much harder than it is today. But a common thread joins both eras together. Tuvaluans survived then just as we do now because of our culture, customs, intelligence, ingenuity and collective ambition. It's true Tuvaluans have adapted, and continue to adapt as best we can.

Here in Tuvalu, subsistence living is still a common way of life, especially in the islands outside the capital, Funafuti. Most people still lack financial or material wealth. Progress has been painstakingly slow in providing modern social services and raising the universal standard of living. Achieving these ends is costly and difficult. But progress of this kind is measured not by the week, but in years and decades and on that score tremendous

progress has been made. Independence was a bold, intrepid step that in the end has proven to be the right one. What was once thought a near impossibility, Tuvaluans have quietly achieved by building a nation. In taking stock, however, the future is filled with challenges and hazards. One hazard in particular poses a dire threat.

A decade ago (and more) we learned that bearing down upon Tuvalu is the prospect of global warming and rising sea levels. We greeted this news with a mixture of worry, fear and dismay. Since then our sense of unease has grown. All island states around the globe, especially the smaller ones like us, share this same emotion and frustration. But it is not just islands that are at risk. Localities as diverse as New Orleans, Venice and the Ganges river delta in south Asia, home to some 60 million people, might partly disappear or vanish without a trace. The vulnerable geography is everywhere. Here in Tuvalu, there is hardly a doubt that a calamity is steadily brewing. The future of Tuvalu is uncertain. Will our land, so obviously at risk, vanish? But Tuvalu's voice in the debate is small, rarely heard, and heeded not at all. Industrial countries, with all their wealth, may fret, but if atmospheric temperatures rise, even a few degrees, the price will be paid by the islands of Tuvalu and all the low-lying land just like it. It may happen.

This book was the idea of a lifelong friend, colleague, and fellow Tuvaluan. I am speaking of the late prime minister, Ionatana Ionatana, who died unexpectedly on 8 December 2000. Known to his friends as John (Ionatana is derived from the English name Jonathan), what he foresaw in this book was a convincing portrayal of Tuvalu, a way to express our concerns and, lastly, a reportage that celebrated life around the country. With that, I have the distinct honour, on behalf of Tuvaluans everywhere, to dedicate *Time & Tide: The Islands of Tuvalu* to the memory of John, the late Ionatana Ionatana.

I inherited from Ionatana the seat of prime minister. Having been bestowed the honour, I am keenly aware that I carry on a legacy that has been moulded year after year, decade after decade, by many Tuvaluans stretching back long before and since independence. What you now hold in your hands provides a glimpse of what I am talking about, a tapestry of contemporary life in Tuvalu.

This book is a gift. In it I hope you sense the loneliness Tuvaluans sometimes feel because of who we are and the vulnerabilities we persistently face, being small in number and living where we do. But what you will see is something much more: Tuvalu's limited but growing prosperity, inherent fragility, the innate hardiness and charm of the Tuvaluan people, and the subtle splendour of each prized atoll. Even for the diaspora, the islands of Tuvalu are nothing less than home.

As we say in our language, *Tuvalu mo te Atua* – Tuvalu for God.

Prime Minister of Tuvalu, the Honourable Faimalaga Luka

Funafuti, June 2001

introduction

By almost every measure Tuvalu is close to the base line. Population? With barely 10,000 people, the Vatican City is virtually the only country with a smaller population. Visitors? Tuvalu's annual 100 to 150 genuine tourists make this one of the world's least visited destinations. Area? The nine islands add up to just 25.6 sq km (10 sq miles) and only two of them – Vaitupu and Nanumea – are larger than New York's Central Park or London's Hampstead Heath. Height? You can climb a palm tree or a church tower, but nowhere does the land reach more than five metres above sea level.

It was Tuvalu's altitude – or rather its distinct lack of altitude – which first brought photographer Peter Bennetts to this scattering of islands. Peter has a keen interest in environmental issues and there's no question that Tuvalu is on the climate-change front line. If the greenhouse effect does lead, as many scientists fear, to rises in sea level then Tuvalu, made up entirely of low-lying coral atolls, could easily be the first country to disappear. Even if it doesn't simply sink beneath the water line, global warming could bring other equally disastrous changes. In 1972 Cyclone Bebe blew right across Funafuti, the capital island, from one side to another, bringing down every house. What sort of a damage could a new 'super storm' wreak on these pancake flat atolls?

Peter's regular visits to Tuvalu led to contact with Prime Minister Ionatana Ionatana. Together they came up with the idea of producing a book about Tuvalu, something which could help to focus attention both on the island nation's story and its troubling challenges.

In late 2000 Peter and I flew to Funafuti. Over the years I have travelled to many other Pacific islands but this was my first visit to the tiny nation. It was Peter's fifth trip and within minutes it was clear that he was a familiar face. We set up shop in the Vaiaku Lagi, Tuvalu's only hotel (Funafuti has a couple of guesthouses and there's a house set aside for visitors on most of the outer islands) and set out to explore the main island in the group. Funafuti is not only home to half the nation's population but also the site of the only working airport. Two other islands have World War II airstrips that are now overgrown with coconut palms.

We boated around Funafuti's lagoon and made a scuba diving foray in the Funafuti Conservation Area, tramped down to the very end of the main island in both directions,

lazed on the beach at Funafala Islet (Funafuti's 'weekend escape'), inspected the Tuvalu Maritime Training Institute and scratched our heads over the garbage piled up in the 'borrow pits'. We even lined up for beers on Twist Night at the raucous Matagigali Bar and unearthed the site of the hole the London Royal Society drilled in 1898 in their attempt to prove Darwin's theory of atoll creation.

Then we boarded the fisheries patrol boat HMTSS *Te Mataili* to make excursions to the other two southern and six northern islands. The *Te Mataili* is one of 22 patrol boats that Australia provides for Pacific nations to chase unlicensed foreign fishing boats that venture into their territorial waters. The patrol boats don't often catch illegal fishermen but they don't need to; their efforts ensure that, these days, most of the north Asian fishing fleets do pay their substantial licensing fees. It's a 'keep them honest' policy which brings in many millions to Pacific island budgets. The *Te Mataili* would drop us off at each island and patrol the local waters while we were onshore.

We visited beautiful Nukulaelae, which is home not only to a monument commemorating the arrival of Christianity in Tuvalu, but also to the best pre-Christian religious site in the nation. On tiny Niulakita, southernmost, smallest and least populated of all the islands, the islanders proved they could turn out a banquet for unexpected visitors at the drop of a hat. We dined on everything from doughnuts with papaya jam to germinating coconuts and, the *pièce de résistance*, smoked noddies. Then we lined up the island's entire population – all 39 of them – for a group photo in front of the church.

Unhappily, our circuit of the southern islands coincided with the unexpected death of the prime minister. Back in Funafuti the funeral was followed by days of bad weather. We were harbour-bound and had to abandon our plans to visit the northern atolls in the group.

Two months later Peter and I were back in Tuvalu, and set off again, this time on the fishing boat *Manaui*. With a visiting film crew we were dropped off on Vaitupu, site of Tuvalu's only secondary school. From there we continued on to Nukufetau where Peter and I stayed while the film crew were ferried back to the main island. Our two-day pause stretched to a week-long wait when the *Manaui* was confined to port with mechanical

problems. It gave us plenty of time to search for wartime relics, reminders of the American air base which operated here during World War II. Luckily, our visit coincided with Tutasi Memorial School Day, the islanders' proud celebration of the establishment of Tuvalu's first primary school. Our nights featured feasting and *fatele*, the Tuvaluans' frenetically energetic dance festivals, as part of the school founding celebrations.

Eventually rescued by the *Te Mataili*, we continued north to the other atolls in the group. Our trip included highlights like a night-time fishing trip to net flying fish off Nanumea. The island's impressive Gothic-style church tower offers the highest viewpoint anywhere in Tuvalu – the only better view would be from an aircraft.

On Nanumaga we waded across the island's shallow, landlocked lagoon and enjoyed an impromptu feast put on by what seemed to be the rowdy women's mat-making circle. On Niutao we were told of island legends ranging from a woman's rain-making abilities to a tragic early encounter between the islanders and visiting Europeans. Finally we turned south and headed back to Funafuti.

Peter had managed to visit all nine atolls in the group and I'd contrived to get to eight of them. We'd been to islands where long stretches may pass between outside visitors, but the Tuvaluans are remarkably mobile people – many of them work on cargo ships – so they're well acquainted with the outside world even if the outside world is much less aware of their tiny nation. We'd seen the problems they struggle with, from overcrowding on densely populated Funafuti to declining populations on some of the smaller islands. We'd listened to their concerns about global climate change and their difficulties with the challenges of the modern world: garbage disposal, alcohol consumption, the change from a subsistence lifestyle to the demands of modern education. We'd seen how, despite these challenges, the Tuvaluan people have managed to build a viable economy by crewing on international cargo ships, by effectively managing the fishing grounds in their huge territorial waters, by building a well-endowed national trust fund managed overseas and, recently, by striking it lucky with their '.tv' Internet domain name. It was a fascinating journey.

vaaitau fakasolo
A BRIEF HISTORY

Very long ago, when there was nothing here but ocean, two friends, Te Pusi (the eel) and Te Ali (the flounder), quarrelled over a magical rock. They fought and Te Ali was wounded, squashed flat like the flounders who now swim in Tuvalu's lagoons. Te Pusi was also transformed in the battle, made long and skinny like an eel. The primordial rock itself was broken into eight pieces, forming the eight atolls of ancient Tuvalu – the name *'tu valu'* means literally 'cluster of eight'.

Long long after this magical battle, people came to Tuvalu. No-one really knows when Tuvalu was first settled – different theories suggest from between 500 and 2000 years ago. The exact route of migration is not known for sure, but one popular theory is that huge voyaging canoes arrived from the south and the east, having spent at least a week sailing the 1000km and more from Samoa, via Tokelau, and Tonga, via Uvéa. Those great canoes would have carried up to a hundred settlers, together with all they would need to populate new lands – coconuts, *pulaka* (taro), pigs and dogs. Tuvalu's first settlers are remembered now in legends such as that of Telematua, the Samoan giant who is said to have settled on Funafuti, Tuvalu's main atoll.

Life on coral atolls is harsh and the new migrants had to adapt quickly, stockpiling food against times of famine and forging intensely close-knit communities. Individual rights tended to be subsumed into the greater good in order that communities could survive. What's more, the Tongans, long after having discovered Tuvalu, continued to visit – but as invaders. Tuvaluans battled invading fleets from both Tonga and Kiribati (their Micronesian neighbours to the north) for centuries. Land was precious to these people – and scarce – so they fought hard to protect it. Not all contact with their neighbours was unfriendly – many 'invaders' stayed on in Tuvalu. In fact one Tongan attack on Funafuti was repelled by two Tuvaluans of I-Kiribati descent, the magical heroes Polau and Salaika.

The culture of Tuvalu today owes something to each of its original settlers – Samoan, Tongan, I-Kiribati and Tokelauan.

After centuries of fending off Tongans and I-Kiribati, not to mention surviving storms, droughts and famine, Tuvalu became known to the rest of the world when the Spaniard Alvaro de Mendaña sailed past in 1568. However, it was another 200 years before the American Arent De Peyster lumbered Funafuti with the unpoetic name 'the Ellice Group' after the English owner of his ship's cargo – the name 'Ellice Islands' was eventually applied to all of Tuvalu.

Tuvalu's resource-poor atolls did not initially spark much interest from the Europeans – no sandalwood to harvest, few whales, difficult anchorages and not enough surplus food to reprovision European ships. Then, in the 1860s, two very different groups discovered two resources that *did* spark interest: bodies and souls.

The 'blackbirders' were first: slave traders who tricked Tuvaluans into boarding their ships or used outright violence then sailed to the guano mines of Peru. Over 400 Tuvaluans disappeared in blackbirders' ships, devastating atolls such as Nukulaelae and Funafuti where two-thirds of the population were taken. None of the kidnapped people ever returned to Tuvalu.

The other group interested in Tuvalu were far more benign, but no less potent: Christian missionaries. A Cook Islands Maori church officer, Elekana, was shipwrecked on Tuvalu en route to Samoa. During his stay Tuvaluans became fascinated by his news of a new religion. (Tragically, this enabled the blackbirders to trick them aboard by posing as missionaries themselves.) Elekana continued on to Samoa, but sent back Samoan-language Bibles and a platoon of other preachers. The missionaries found Tuvaluans keen to embrace the new religion and set to work distributing Bibles, baptising so-called 'heathens', supervising the

building of churches and, sadly, destroying pre-Christian idols and temples. Christianity came to dominate Tuvalu – the old gods were dead and missionaries replaced *tofuga* (priests) as primary advisers to the *aliki* (chiefs) on each atoll. Today, Tuvalu is one of the most devoutly Christian nations on Earth.

With Christianity established in Tuvalu, trade with European nations increased markedly and the fleets of many Western nations prowled this section of the Pacific looking for whales, trade or strategic advantage. Eventually the British, with economic interests to protect, took neighbouring Kiribati (then known as the Gilbert Islands) as a protectorate, and proposed to include Tuvaluans as part of the new 'Protectorate of the Gilbert & Ellice Islands'. Tuvaluans were far from united in their desire to become new Britons, but eventually, in 1892, Funafuti's high chief, Elia, a direct descendent of the legendary Telematua, signed on the dotted line and Tuvalu became the newest (and perhaps smallest) fragment of the British Empire.

During Tuvalu's time as a British protectorate, and later as a fully fledged British colony, there was at least plenty of opportunity for work – in the phosphate mines of Kiribati's Ocean Island – although the work was arduous, conditions were dangerous and the pay was lousy. Also during this time a competent local government was set up – one that provided vital experience for Tuvaluans when they eventually gained independence.

As World War II raged across the Pacific, in October 1942 an American convoy sailed into the Funafuti Lagoon and proceeded to turn the island into a military base – quickly constructing Funafuti's airfield, which involved clearing much of the island's swamps, *pulaka* pits and coconut plantations. From their strategic location in Tuvalu, American aircraft were able to bomb Japanese bases in Kiribati, Nauru and the Marshall Islands. There were more than 6000 Americans in Tuvalu at the peak of the Pacific campaign, but by the end of 1944 the conflict had moved north and the bases in Tuvalu were emptying even before the war ended. Many reminders of those times remain – from bomb shelters and the remains of downed bombers to World War II–era Coke bottles used as decorations on graves.

Soon after the war, Tuvalu, the 'cluster of eight', became a cluster of nine. The British colonial authorities decided that Niutao, Tuvalu's most densely populated atoll, needed more space and shipped a party of Niutao islanders down to uninhabited Niulakita Atoll. There, to the surprise of all concerned, it was discovered another group, from Vaitupu Island, had already moved in! The Vaitupuans were unceremoniously shipped back to Vaitupu and Niulakita Atoll has remained a Niutao fief ever since. With nine atolls now populated, there was a brief debate about changing the traditional name to 'Tuiva' (cluster of nine) but it never took hold.

As the smaller cousins in the union of the Gilbert & Ellice Islands Tuvaluans always felt that their interests were secondary to the more populous I-Kiribati. When Kiribati sought independence in the 1960s (eventually to become the Republic of Kiribati in 1979), the Tuvaluans decided to go their separate way. The independent nation of Tuvalu was formed on 1 October 1978.

The Pacific's newest nation, however, was poor. With few resources other than fish and coconuts the Tuvaluan government and people struggled, heavily dependent on foreign aid for their schools, health services and other infrastructure. This all began to change in the late 1990s. Being a frugal people by nature, over the years the Tuvaluan government amassed sizeable cash reserves, that is, savings from the Tuvaluan Trust Fund, fish licensing fees and other sources of income. To top it off the government of Tuvalu struck a deal to license the country's top-level domain name, the two-letter suffix at the end of their national Internet address, '.tv'. That deal guarantees Tuvalu US$4 million per year up to US$50 million – a very significant sum for a country whose previous annual national budgets seldom exceeded US$5 million. This new income, combined with national savings, is being used to repair roads, improve standards of health and, that most important of Tuvaluan priorities, education. Tuvalu is being very careful with its new-found wealth. There are no grand plans, just a careful investment strategy to ensure that the money will last.

Tuvaluans know that they face challenging times ahead. If even the most conservative of greenhouse-effect predictions are true, Tuvalu will need funds to offset storm damage and loss of fisheries. Ultimately, Tuvaluans will need to purchase land – somewhere – to replace their atolls if they disappear beneath the rising seas.

The greenhouse effect is the issue that dominates Tuvalu's future. In fact there's a very real possibility that as the greenhouse effect takes a grip on the world's climate over the next century, Tuvalu could cease to exist altogether.

Tu mo aganuu, talitonuga faka te agaaga mote akoga atiakega fakavae
o Tuvalu ite vaaitau

'Culture, faith and education are the foundation of modern Tuvalu' (former prime minister Ionatana Ionatana in a speech to the United Nations)

Eighty-eight year old Kelese Simona lives on Nukulaelae, the atoll known in Tuvalu as 'The Land of the Beautiful Woman of the Sunrise'. But Nukulaelae's poetic name belies a dark past. In 1863, most of the population of Nukulaelae Atoll was kidnapped by Peruvian slave traders, called 'blackbirders'. Kelese's father told him about the blackbirders: 'A ship turned up outside the lagoon and invited the people on board to eat, sing and dance, but they were lying. Once the people were on board they locked them up and sailed away. Two men escaped and swam back to shore but the rest were never seen again.'

Men and boys boarded first, enticed by promises of feasting and dancing, then sent back word to the women of

'Once the people were on board they locked them up and sailed away. Two men escaped and swam back to shore but the rest were never seen again.'

Nukulaelae to join them. The Peruvian slave traders sailed off with 250 men, women and children, intending to sell them to work excavating guano from islands off the South American coast. Of those kidnapped, most were dead within a few years; none lived to see Tuvalu again. Fewer than 100 people were left on Nukulaelae Atoll.

Elia Tavita is the *pule o kaupule*, the council president for Funafuti Atoll. He heads the busiest council in Tuvalu. Funafuti, the nation's capital, is the most populated of Tuvalu's atolls – almost half the country's population lives there.

The size of that population is Funafuti's biggest problem. 'We have little land,' Elia says. 'Waste management is a big problem.' And the problem keeps growing as more and more Tuvaluans relocate from the other atolls to Funafuti: 'Jobs are easier to get here than on the outer islands. Young people come here to the bright lights – that sort of thing.'

Elia achieved local fame years ago when he helped apprehend the crew of a Korean boat that was illegally fishing in Tuvalu's waters. Elia, who was out

'Jobs are easier to get here than on the outer islands. Young people come here to the bright lights — that sort of thing.'

fishing with his cousin, was asked by the crew whether they could buy bananas. 'Follow me into the lagoon and I'll guide you to the town – there's plenty of bananas there,' he told them. Once ashore the gullible crew were arrested by police and charged.

tuu mo aganu tuvalu

TRADITIONAL TUVALUAN CUSTOMS & CULTURE

Ancient Tuvalu was egalitarian compared with many Polynesian societies; a fairly 'flat' hierarchy dominated everyday life. There was no overall ruler of Tuvalu, but each atoll had its own 'high chief', or *ulu aliki*. Below him (the *ulu aliki* was invariably a man) sub-chiefs *(aliki)* ruled the villages with the assistance of an island council of elders (*te sina o fenua* – literally, the island's 'grey-hairs') and priests *(tofuga)*. When Tongans, I-Kiribati or other Tuvaluans threatened, the *aliki* had an order of warriors to fall back on. Other Tuvaluan commoners concentrated on different areas of responsibility – each family specialising in one task such as boat building, fishing or growing *pulaka* (taro). Family knowledge was guarded fiercely. Below everyone else there were the slaves, usually unfortunates who had been captured in war and the first 'under the knife' if the *tofuga* determined that the gods needed mollifying.

In modern Tuvalu the roles of *aliki* and *ulu aliki* are largely ceremonial, but in practice they wield considerable power. The official leader of an atoll now is the *pule o kaupule*, or president, the person who leads the *kaupule*, or island council. Council business is still conducted in the *falekaupule* (village meeting hall). The *falekaupule* is an ancient tradition; it's used for everything from village meetings to wedding receptions, funerals, dances and welcoming feasts, and its cultural importance is signified by its image on Tuvalu's coat of arms.

On outer atolls, the *kaupule* is vastly more influential than the national government, hundreds of kilometres across the sea at Funafuti. If conflict arises between the *kaupule* elders and, say, young Tuvaluans who have travelled overseas, seen a bit of the world, and returned with fancy modern ideas about individuality, you can be sure the elders will prevail! *Kaupule* members are now elected rather than appointed on the basis of age, but they still tend to be the village's elders. In some ways, Tuvalu has hardly changed at all.

When ancient Tuvaluans adapted to life on these atolls they quickly found consensus and unity were the only ways to survive. Dissent and confrontation were contrary to that way of life. It's not that individuality isn't permitted, but it must be balanced with the community's needs. The *kaupule* are the ones who decide how to handle that balance. Today the village priest fills the role of the vanished *tofuga* in advising the *kaupule*. There are still remnants of ancient Tuvaluan spiritualism in some aspects of Tuvaluan culture, but the majority of the people are Christian.

Once key Tuvaluan elders and chiefs adopted Christianity at the end of the 19th century, the religion spread like wildfire. (Niutao was perhaps the only exception, clinging to its traditional religion long after the other atolls had capitulated.) Religious dissent certainly did not fit into the strict Tuvaluan community life, where unity is paramount, so after a critical mass had embraced Christianity, dissenters were liable to be forcibly persuaded. These days unity is no longer quite so strictly enforced, and the Protestant Church of Tuvalu now competes with Roman Catholics, Seventh Day Adventists, Jehovah's Witnesses and Baha'i. Funafuti even has a small mosque. But it's the Protestant Church, and the churches themselves, that get the most attention. In fact Tuvalu's motto, *Tuvalu mo te Atua*, means 'Tuvalu is for God'.

On any Tuvaluan atoll the church is likely to be the largest, most elaborate structure. In stark contrast to the small, temporary-looking homes, churches, built by community workgroups, are solid, well built and well patronised. On Sunday mornings in Tuvalu today you won't see many people on the streets, unless, dressed in their best blinding white or brightest colours, they're on their way to church. The largest and most impressive of the nation's churches is Nanumea Atoll's Gothic-inspired turreted masterpiece – about 20m tall, it's four times taller than the highest point of land in all of Tuvalu!

An aspect of Tuvaluan society that was introduced by the missionaries, and one that at first glance seems to go against the principle of communal unity, is the division of each village population into two *feitu* ('sides' or 'teams'). Every member of the community belongs to one *feitu* or the other, and the two *feitu* compete against each other in many

aspects of village life, from community building projects to fishing, to sports such as soccer or *kilikiti* (Tuvaluan cricket), to the central feature of Tuvaluan social life, the *fatele*, or competitive dance. People can relocate to the other side of the village but they always retain membership in their *feitu*. It's similar in the Tuvaluan population of Fiji's Kioa Island, settled from Tuvalu's Vaitupu in 1946, where the old folk still call themselves Vaitupuans. No matter where you live now, the land and home of your ancestors determines who you are.

Polynesians value land above all else – even more, perhaps, here in Tuvalu, where land is so scarce. At least, unlike some ex-colonies, in Tuvalu the people still own the land. Money, as 19th-century Western traders soon discovered, may be able to buy many things but in Tuvalu it cannot buy land. It simply isn't for sale. There's a saying in Tuvalu: 'Money is for *palagi* (Europeans) and land is for Tuvaluans'. In fact the Tuvaluan language gives several insights into the way Tuvaluans think about land. For example, in Tuvaluan, a person who doesn't own land is known as *fakaalofa* – literally, a person deserving of pity and charity. The word *fenua* is another example – the same word means both the land itself, and the people who live on that land. Thus *te sina o fenua*, the old name for island councils, meant both the island's elders (grey-hairs), and the people's elders.

'Sa fia Eulopa ia koe e mativa kae tuapuu'

'If you copy palagi ways you are poor and unhealthy' (from a traditional Tuvaluan song)

Malaki Mauga is the *ulu aliki*, or high chief, on Nukulaelae Atoll.

In the past each atoll had an *ulu aliki*, selected from all the island chiefs. The *ulu aliki* was the man with the last word when there were decisions to be made. These days the *ulu aliki* is still chosen from the hereditary island chiefs, but his power is now shared with another man on each atoll, the *pule o kaupule*, or elected village president. In practice, the two men must work together – balancing the needs of traditional Tuvalu and modern Tuvalu.

Malaki Mauga is also a master boat builder. Over the years he's made perhaps 20 canoes, the first of them when he was about 30 years old. The dugout canoe he's working on right now has taken

The *ulu aliki* was the man with the last word when there were decisions to be made.

about two weeks to carve to this stage. The hull has been roughed out from a breadfruit tree using a chainsaw but the fine work will be done by hand, using an adze. This canoe is for Aifou Tafie, Nukulaelae's *kaupule* president.

Seono Paneva, 81 years old, is a village elder on enigmatic Niutao, an island where the people retain many traditional, pre-Christian beliefs and customs.

Seono is a master of an ancient Tuvaluan form of martial arts which includes use of *katipopuki* (hardwood spears) such as the one he now holds. This particular dark, lethal-looking spear is at least 100 years old and features in a story that Seono Paneva tells. 'They bathed in the well,' he says, the sheer outrage at this craven display of bad manners evident in his tone. 'So my ancestors speared them and this *katipopuki* was what they used.'

The well lies just south of the high *pulaka* (taro) pit wall in the centre of the island. Here, long ago, five *palagi* (European) visitors had the bad manners to bathe in the precious water and were

'They bathed in the well, so my ancestors speared them and this *katipopuki* was what they used.'

attacked by the incensed islanders. One of the women was speared and killed while the rest of the intruders were bound and thrown in the sea to drown.

Later their bodies were washed ashore and they were buried in a small cemetery just east of the village.

When Seono Paneva tells the story of the massacre, though, you can't help feeling that he doesn't think his ancestors overreacted at all.

Tubwebwe Teoli was born in Tuvalu's northern neighbour, Kiribati, but she has lived in Tuvalu for 11 years and is married to a Tuvaluan man here on Nukulaelae Atoll. She has three children ranging in age from 13 to 20 and feels quite at home in Tuvalu.

Life is quiet here 'in the bush', says Tubwebwe. Indeed it would be hard to find anywhere quieter than Tubwebwe's home. Nukulaelae Atoll is Tuvalu's second-most southern and second-least populated atoll, but Tubwebwe lives right out on the edge of the village.

Tubwebwe is the island expert on traditional medicine and knows many uses for the plants that grow on the island. *Nonu*, the fruit which has become a modest craze in the West in recent

'There's no difference between being married to a Tuvaluan man or an I-Kiribati man', she reports. 'They're all men.'

years, is part of her medical arsenal. The juice squeezed from *nonu* fruit is strained through a white cloth, mixed with water and drunk immediately. It's a popular cure for asthma. Pandanus root is another natural medicine. When crushed and mixed with coconut leaves it is a cure for fever in small children. Grated coconut and the inner part of the pandanus leaf works wonders for people suffering from fish poisoning.

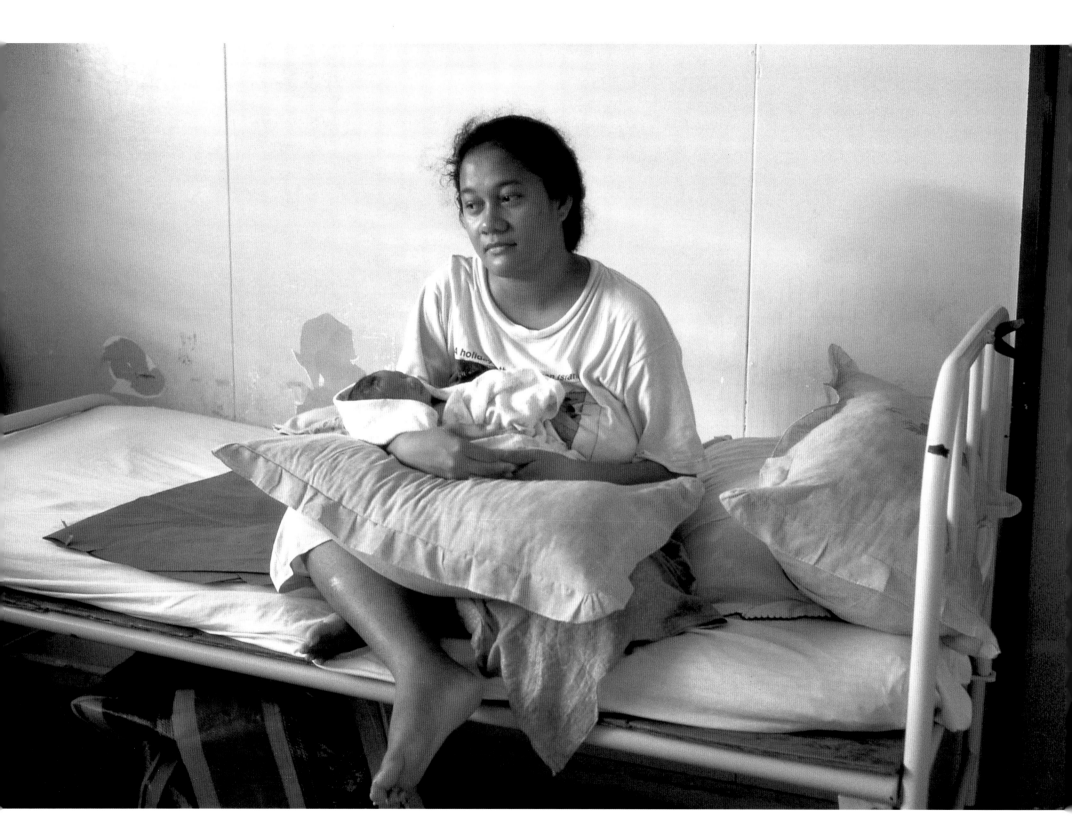

Terube Alinesi is a nurse working at the medical centre on Nui Atoll. Although Tuvalu is a Polynesian country, the people of Nui also claim Micronesian ancestors (settlers from Kiribati). I-Kiribati arrived in Nui in successive waves more than a hundred years ago after most of the original Polynesian settlers had fled from famine. The story goes (if the history is reliable), the I-Kiribati invaders killed most of the men and took the women as wives.

Terube herself is a much later arrival from Kiribati. After training as a nurse she worked for a time on Nauru. There she met her Tuvaluan husband, who was working in the phosphate mine. They moved here together 16 years ago.

Nui's medical staff constantly battle isolation. Medical supplies can run out whenever storms or mechanical trouble delay the inter-island ship, *Nivaga II*. If a

'This year a woman died and the baby was inside. She was bleeding. It was an antepartum haemorrhage. The patrol boat was too late and she died.'

patient urgently needs specialised treatment at Tuvalu's only hospital (Funafuti Atoll), or in Suva (Fiji), they have to wait until a boat can reach them. Even relatively minor problems can be life threatening on Tuvalu's outer atolls. 'Sometimes there are problems with childbirth,' Terube says. 'This year a woman died and the baby was inside. She was bleeding. It was an antepartum haemorrhage. The patrol boat was too late and she died.'

Akoakoga Kalala is Nanumea Atoll's third police officer and one of six female police officers in Tuvalu. She joined the police force on Funafuti Atoll right after she finished school at the age of 17 and came home to Nanumea after a couple of years' service in the capital.

'Traffic offences are the main crime,' she says.

That seems scarcely credible when the atoll's vehicle fleet seems to consist of one battered truck, the government office's tractor and a handful of motorcycles, but it seems young Nanumeans have a habit of jumping on board a relative's motorcycle without first getting a driving licence. A glance through the police station's record book indicates that failing to keep your property tidy and letting your pigs get loose are equally frequent infringements of the law.

'It's a peaceful place,' Akoakoga says, and reflects that the restrictions on the sale of alcohol probably play a large part in that peace. On a small atoll you tend to live in each other's pockets and the people here know they can't get away with much. Night-time break-ins – and there aren't many of those – are generally the only unsolved crime.

Tuvalu has only one prison; it's located on Funafuti. Since there's nowhere much to go if you escape, security is not a big issue, and you're likely to find one of the five inmates sitting out front doing the laundry.

A glance through the police station's record book indicates that failing to keep your property tidy and letting your pigs get loose are equally frequent infringements of the law.

One internee is rather colourful. Posing as a Singaporean businessman the visitor announced he had come to Tuvalu to set up a joint venture business enterprise. He settled into the Vaiaku Lagi Hotel and dropped round to the bank to cash US$2000 in travellers cheques. A few days later he returned to the bank with US$47,000. This seemed a suspiciously large sum to officials at the bank and, sure enough, the cheques turned out to be fakes. So did the 'businessman's' Singapore credentials. He turned out to be from Shanghai – but reportedly his time in the Funafuti clink has convinced him that the Pacific might not be a bad place to settle down once he has served his sentence.

salaaga ote atamai
A BETTER LIFE

'Culture, faith and education are the foundation of modern Tuvalu.' So said the late Ionatana Ionatana to the United Nations in Tuvalu's introductory speech – publicly proclaiming the importance of education to his people. From primary school to secondary and higher, Tuvaluans are willing to make great sacrifices for their education.

Primary school students may not be expected to make great sacrifices themselves – in fact the life of very young Tuvaluans is remarkably clear of stress or responsibility – but the entire community is expected to support their children's education. Primary schools are invariably built by village-wide communal teams, and woe betide anyone who thinks they've got something better to do with their time than help fit the roof to the new classroom. Lasting pride is taken in the results of these labours – for example, on 11 February each year Nukufetau Atoll celebrates the founding of its beloved Tutasi Memorial School, the first primary school in Tuvalu, with a parade, class performances and two days of *fatele* (dance).

There's only one secondary school in Tuvalu – Motufoua School on Vaitupu. Students from the other eight atolls have to leave their families and homes for the long school terms to board here on Vaitupu. It is at once a heart-breaking moment and a cause for great excitement when Tuvalu's one inter-island ship, *Nivaga II*, collects students from their home atolls to take them to Vaitupu.

The special place Motufoua School holds in the hearts of Tuvaluans was tragically highlighted in March 2000 when a young girl, studying late at night, knocked over a candle and set her bedding on fire. It might have been a minor mishap if the doors to the dormitory had not been locked and the windows barred. As it was, 18 teenage girls and their matron were killed; in a country of less than 10,000 people it was an overwhelming tragedy. Then prime minister, Ionatana Ionatana, cancelled an official trip to Hawaii to visit the school (a six-hour boat trip from Funafuti Atoll) and declared a national day of mourning. On many Tuvaluan islands, from Vaitupu itself to tiny Nukulaelae, you will see memorials to students killed in the fire. Tuvaluans treasure their youth; to lose 18 of them to the school fire was a catastrophe.

Until very recently, families were expected to contribute towards their children's secondary schooling at Motufoua. Now, however, with income coming into Tuvalu from The .tv Corporation Internet venture and other sources, the government has been able to abolish school fees. A long-term dream to make schooling free for all has finally been accomplished. The

government always said that education would be the first to benefit from The .tv Corporation revenue – in fact education, along with sports and culture, is the largest beneficiary of core government expenditure.

Tuvaluans who wish to go on to tertiary education must leave Tuvalu – usually to attend universities in Fiji, New Zealand or Australia. There are strong Tuvaluan communities in those countries, and the students are both cared for and closely monitored by their countryfolk, but it is still a long, long way from the loving embrace of family in Tuvalu. And once educated young Tuvaluans return home, they might find that Tuvalu is a long, long way from the nightclubs and cafe culture of Suva, Auckland or Sydney!

A much more common destination, for young men at least, is the Tuvalu Maritime Training Institute on Amatuku Islet, Funafuti. About 60 Tuvaluans every year graduate from the Training Institute as sailors, and at any given moment there are about 450 Tuvaluan sailors out on the high seas, with another 250 to 300 on home leave. Tuvaluan sailors are in great demand on international, mostly German, cargo ships, favoured for their reputation as hard workers and for the strong community spirit that a team of Tuvaluans develops on a ship at sea. The sailors' income is an important part of the Tuvaluan economy –

contributing about US$3 million annually. Agencies back on Funafuti handle the money paid to the sailors, sending an agreed proportion to families on various atolls. In any Tuvaluan village, income from sailors is probably the greatest difference between the haves and the have-nots. For the young sailors it's hard work but satisfying. Perhaps the greatest problem is the culture shock that comes when a well-travelled man of the world returns to his quiet home atoll for a holiday with the folks. Just try explaining to Mum and Dad that you've got out of the habit of attending church on Sundays!

I sose aso e tusa mose 450 kauvaka Tuvalu e taape solo i vasa ote lalolagi

On any given day there are about 450 Tuvaluan sailors out on the high seas

taafaaooga
AT PLAY

There are plenty of ways to pass the time in Tuvalu – picnics, sports, card games, 'twist nights' at the hotel or just watching TV. And that doesn't even include the dancing and feasting. It seems that almost anything will do as an excuse for a *fatele*, the Tuvaluan word for a dance, and if you're dancing, you might as well be feasting!

A festival is a conventional reason for a *fatele*. It might be an official national holiday such as the Queen's Birthday (the Queen of England of course) or Independence Day. It might be a Christian festival such as Easter or Christmas. Or it might be a local holiday such as Bomb Day – commemorating the day in 1943 when the Japanese airforce bombed Funafuti's church, narrowly missing the villagers. Equally, a *fatele* might be called to celebrate a wedding, or to mark the end of a community project such as the building of a new classroom or church, or to welcome important visitors to the atoll, or to celebrate any visitors to the tiny outer atolls which receive so few! Or, if no reason for *fatele* presents itself, Tuvaluans might just hold one anyway.

Once the decision has been made that it's time for a *fatele*, all the people of a village will assemble – usually in the *falekaupule* (village hall). The population of a Tuvaluan village is divided into two *feitu* ('sides' or 'teams') and the members of each *feitu* take up station at opposite ends of the *falekaupule*. The two *feitu* will perform in turn. A *fatele* is not just a session of community music, singing and dancing – it is a very competitive event!

In the centre of each *feitu*, men sit around a large, rectangular, wooden drum, thumping it with the palms of their hands or wooden sticks to produce the background beat. Another man drums on a metal cabin cracker tin, creating a wonderfully noisy racket. Around this central group of musicians the singers, male and female, sit cross-legged. The rhythm starts gently and builds, the tempo getting faster and faster, the drumming louder and louder until it peaks in a thumping, crashing crescendo. The singing follows suit, starting gently and harmoniously and building to a full-throated melange of harmonies and counter-harmonies. The word *fatele* means 'to multiply', hinting at that steadily increasing speed.

To one side of the musicians and singers are the dancers, a group of women with flowers wreathing their heads and brown grass skirts circling their waists. Occasionally a male dancer may jump up to do a short warrior-like bent-leg dance, but it's generally left to the women to sway statuesquely until ending their dance with a graceful twirl as if to say 'So beat that!'

Which is precisely what the other side tries to do.

Feitu, village 'sides', are also useful when selecting teams for more traditional sports. Most sports played in Tuvalu would be recognisable to the casual observer – for example the 'world game', soccer, a legacy of Tuvalu's time as a British colony. However, even the world game must adapt to the local environment: There's not much flat land available on Tuvalu, certainly not enough to waste it on soccer fields, so on Funafuti the game is often played on the airport runway. Planes arrive only twice per week so they very rarely interrupt games. The airfield is too large to fence off from the island's huge dog population, always eager to join in the action, but a good swift kick prevents canine pitch invasions.

Another Tuvaluan favourite, *kilikiti* (cricket), is even further removed from its origins. Split, again, into the two *feitu*, participants follow rules that are recognisable from English cricket, but with important differences. Most noticeably, the game has expanded far beyond eleven-a-side to include as many people as want to play – and that can be pretty much everyone in the village! The batter isn't required to run; instead there's a dedicated runner, so the batter can concentrate on whacking the ball with the three-sided bat, a cross between a baseball bat and a war club. The shape of the bat ensures that the ball flies off pretty much at random. As well as the players themselves, other members of the *feitu*

attend to sing and dance at appropriate times – both in support of their *feitu* and to taunt the other side.

A distinctly Tuvaluan sport is *ano*. To play *ano* you need two round balls about 12cm in diameter, woven from dried pandanus leaves. The two opposing teams face each other about 7m apart in five or six parallel rows of about six people, and nominate a captain *(alovaka)* and a catcher *(tino pukepuke)* who stand in front of each team. Team members can hit the ball to each other with the aim of eventually reaching the catcher. Only the catcher can throw the ball back to the captain to hit back to the other team. To keep the game lively, two balls are used simultaneously. When either ball falls to the ground the other team scores a point and the first to ten points wins the game. *Ano* is played less and less often these days. Although it seems a game is always just about to start, it never does. Naturally, any sporting tournament, whether soccer, *kilikiti*, *ano*, volleyball or rugby, is invariably followed by *fatele* and feasting. In many cases there's not a clear distinction between work and play in Tuvalu. Many vital tasks are done in such a way that you can't believe the workers begrudge the work. Take fishing for example. If the fish weren't needed to put dinner on the table, you suspect the men would be out there catching them anyway!

Se fakamasakoga fua o fai se fatele...

Any excuse for a fatele...

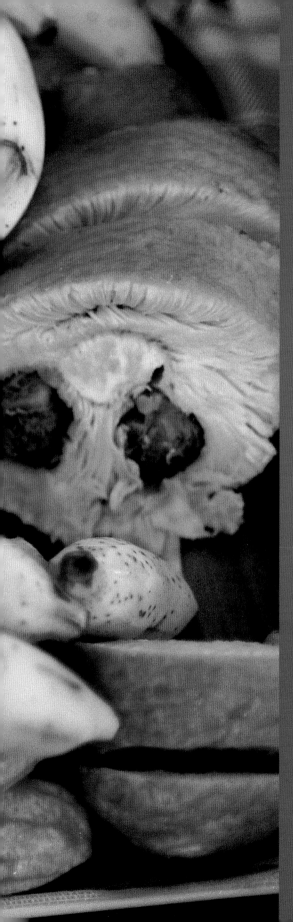

fakaala samu eiloa
FEASTING FROM THE SEA

Tuvaluans love their food, perhaps because, in the past, food supplies were not always guaranteed. In fact food on these small and densely populated atolls could be frighteningly scarce at times. Frequent cyclones and droughts could wipe out months of supplies. Even now, cyclones, droughts and, more prosaically, delays in the inter-island shipping schedule, can leave outer atolls short of foodstuffs. The only resource that's (almost) guaranteed is fish.

As poor as they are in land resources, Tuvalu's atolls are rich in seafood. Tuvaluans ply coastal waters and lagoons for seafood in small canoes and motorboats. It can be a dangerous way to gain food – fishermen have been lost at sea when sudden squalls appear, or they find themselves out of sight of the low-lying atolls or their outboard motors fail and they drift out to sea.

The Tuvaluan diet is a fairly simple one, and in some ways very traditional. Fish is the major source of protein, along with crabs and turtles; bananas and breadfruit are other staples, and there are always coconuts to eat and drink. *Pulaka*, a taro-like plant, is the principal starch food of the islands. It is grown in enormous pits, which are painstakingly produced over many generations, excavated down to the water table and filled with composted soil. At the southern end of Nanumaga Atoll are probably the highest 'hills' to be found anywhere in Tuvalu. They're totally artificial, the result of these deep excavations. The traditional quest for food has resulted in certain rules: on Niulakita nobody is allowed to shout or sing if they're walking through the interior as it frightens the birds who are an important part of the island diet; and you mustn't show lights at night because it could scare away turtles.

But the traditional diet is now supplemented by preserved, canned food imported from abroad. The *fusi* is the village store, the place to pick up a sack of rice or a can of corned beef and to catch up on island gossip while you're shopping. Along with the *falekaupule* (village hall) and the church, the *fusi* is a feature on every island (except tiny Niulakita). *Fusi* are communally owned shops which provide goods at a lower cost to the islanders, and give them a better price for their own produce. They sidestep a particularly Polynesian problem associated with individually owned shops. The cultural importance of sharing is so overriding that even today it is difficult for an islander to operate a retail business. If you've got goods on the shelves surely your friends and relatives deserve a share of them? And if they need something how can you possibly charge them money? It's a capitalist necessity that shops have to make money. But by transferring that need from the individual to the community the *fusi* made it possible for shops to be operated by islanders, not solely by outsiders who operate shops on many Pacific islands.

Today cosmopolitan Funafuti has a number of other shops as well, but on most other islands the *fusi* is the only shopping outlet. And it's nothing like a 7-Eleven. Goods are often scattered indiscriminately across the floor; what appears on the shelves often bears little relationship to what might be stacked under the counter or in the stockroom; cans are often old and rusty; the displays are generally old behind-the-counter rather than modern supermarket style; there's surprisingly little local produce and finding something that doesn't taste stale is pure luck. In the older shops you have to ask for each item, which is then collected from the shelves and handwritten in a ledger before the next item is fetched. It's no wonder there's plenty of time for local gossip in a *fusi* queue.

The drawback is that the heavily processed food leads to health problems such as obesity and diabetes – as citizens of affluent countries know all too well. And in land-deficient Tuvalu, where rubbish can't be tucked away out of sight as it is in most countries, all those empty packets, cans and bottles constitute a large, unsightly environmental problem. Finish drinking a coconut and it's soon compost; toss away a soft drink can and it's there for a half-century. The problem is most evident on Funafuti because not only does it have the most people but it also has the people who have most to throw away. There's a good chance

Funafuti could submerge under its garbage long before it submerges under sea water.

Sour toddy, or fermented coconut sap, is the standard local alcoholic drink. On Funafuti sour toddy is now severely challenged by beer, but beer has caused problems and most of the other atolls have banned it. As Niulakita's pastor Alafaio Honolulu explains, 'It makes your head go round and round,' and then 'the turtles will not come'.

The simplicity of the Tuvaluan diet is turned on its head when there's a feast; that's when the Tuvaluan love for food is given free expression. Feasts are invariably held in the island *falekaupule*, and accompanied by *fatele* (dance), singing and long, long speeches. A local maxim is 'There's no such thing as a short speech in Tuvaluan'.

When a feast is planned, local fishermen are on a mission to catch more fish than ever before, the *pulaka* pits and coconut trees are raided, bananas are stewed in toddy and papayas made into jam. Coconut crabs are hauled from their burrows, birds are lured down from the sky and netted to be smoked or grilled, and local pigs are doomed. For most of the year Tuvalu's pigs are raised in seaside pens, where they live a happy if demoralised life – or, if they're clever enough, escape to run around the village wreaking havoc and making entertainment for children. But when it's feasting time, pork is the centre of the menu.

Ka fai ko fakatoka se fakaala, ko taa mai ei a pulaka, fakanamu mai a uu, fakatagi
a seu manu kae suki mai foki tei mote puaka

When a feast is planned pulaka *pits are raided, coconuts crabs are hauled from their burrows, birds are lured down from the sky, and local pigs are doomed*

Sixty-three-year-old Tepoutoa Epati is a 'birdcaller', possibly Vaitupu's best bird-caller and certainly its busiest and most experienced. Tepoutoa has been calling birds for more than 40 years.

Vaitupu has about 30 birdcallers, practitioners of a uniquely Tuvaluan method of bird hunting. Birdcallers shimmy to the top of tall trees where they imitate birds with loud calls. When the birds follow the call to the tree they are snared in large, long-handled nets. Several types of seabirds are caught this way – *taketake* (black noddies), and *akiaki* (white terns) are favourites. Grilled or smoked, the *taketake* are a Tuvaluan delicacy.

Tepoutoa catches about 10 to 20 birds a day from 'his' tree. Each birdcaller has their own favourite tree, selected for

'I prepared the tree for my own use,' he says. 'You must carefully select the right place for the birds. You don't just see a beautiful *puka* that is easy to climb and go there.'

its position and height and chopped with an axe for ease of climbing. Tepoutoa has been using the same *puka* tree for 20 years. 'I prepared the tree for my own use,' he says. 'You must carefully select the right place for the birds. You don't just see a beautiful *puka* that is easy to climb and go there. You have to survey. You have to know where the birds come in from the sea. You have to find a tree in the right spot.'

'It's pitch black; the boat is moving fast; all eyes are concentrating on the fish.'

Rising almost vertically, a flying fish stalls and drops straight down into the boat. Others, zooming across the boat, hit the fishermen themselves with a wet 'thwack' and also fall into the boat.

Chasing flying fish has always been both a productive means of food gathering and rip-roaring good fun.

The technique is simple but effective: On a dark, moonless night, take a powerful outboard-powered boat and three men; one piloting the boat, a second sitting Buddha-like perched on the very bow of the boat and wielding what looks like a large, very strong butterfly net, and a second netman sitting between them amidships. The netman at the bow wears a miner's helmet, with a powerful spotlight strapped above his forehead.

The boat speeds along, the spotlight scares up the fish which, as flying fish do, take to the air, and the two netmen simply scoop them up in mid-flight. If the fishermen look skilled and practised, that's because Tuvaluans have been catching flying fish this way for a long time. In the old days the boat would have been an outrigger canoe, the power would have been provided by muscular paddlers and the light would have come from burning palm fronds, but the end result is still the same.

Unfortunately for both the flying fish and fishermen, hungry dolphins join in the fun – they race in front of the boat, leaping out of the water to grab more than their fair share of flying fish. In the moonless night the dolphins are mere dark shapes flashing through the water, but you can clearly hear them breathing as they leap through the water ahead, behind and to either side of the boat. The result is a scene of sheer, exuberant chaos: the boat tearing along through the darkness, the only light coming from a spotlight that whips off in all directions as the lead netman twists to net a fish, all three fishermen yelling and screaming at one another in their excitement, dolphins leaping and a maelstrom of flying fish ricocheting in all directions. It is not uncommon for a fisherman to receive a blow to the head from a flying fish in flight.

There's a final stationary ingredient in the mix. For the best fishing the boat must run parallel to the atoll coastline and close to the reef edge. *Very* close! It's pitch black; the boat is moving fast; all eyes are concentrating on the fish – it would be all too easy to run into the reef. Somehow it doesn't happen – there are some close calls, but an hour later the fishermen head home with a boat full of flying fish. No doubt the dolphins have done well for themselves too.

Laki Kalapu is a fisherman. He used to fish the deep seas outside Funafuti Atoll's fringing coral reef – but now he uses hand-held nets to catch the smaller fish close to shore. The reason Laki can't fish the high seas anymore is because he had to abandon his small boat the *Fetu te Moana* (the star of the sea) after he accidentally ended up on Futuna a few years ago. He had been fishing offshore with another man when his engine died and the boat was blown out to sea. They drifted for over a month, and survived on rainwater and what fish they could catch, dried in the sun. One day there was a knock on the side of the boat and when Laki looked over there was a turtle. 'Thank you, God,' he said, before pulling it on board, killing and eating it.

One day there was a knock on the side of the boat and when Laki looked over there was a turtle. 'Thank you, God,' he said, before pulling it aboard, killing it and eating it.

That wasn't the first time Laki had got lost at sea. A year earlier he had sailed the *Fetu te Moana* too far out to sea after his quarry and lost sight of low-lying Funafuti. That time he drifted almost two months and ended up 1000km away in American Samoa. Perhaps it's best if Laki sticks to using a net.

seaa nei te iumanai
AN UNCERTAIN FUTURE

Tuvalu's environment shapes its people's lives. The atolls on which Tuvaluans live are invariably small, isolated and poor in resources, even such basic resources as soil, fresh water and timber. But the overwhelming feature that a visitor notes, and the feature that puts Tuvalu's very existence at risk, is the low profile of the atolls. Nowhere in Tuvalu does the land rise more than 5m above sea level, and with sea levels predicted to rise a metre or more in the next hundred years, Tuvalu may be one of the first countries to be rendered uninhabitable by the runaway 'greenhouse effect' and climate change.

They're popular scientific buzz words, and their causes are well known. We've been pouring harmful gases into the atmosphere, thereby increasing the proportion of carbon dioxide, leading to temperature increases. These increases are accelerated as we destroy the planet's vegetation cover and so reduce its ability to consume carbon dioxide. It's not simply that the sea level rise from melting polar ice caps will inundate a large part of Tuvalu's tiny land area; the problem is compounded by the slowly rising saltwater table below the atolls, which is already poisoning deep-rooted crops such as *pulaka* (taro) and coconut. In addition, increased sea temperatures will slowly kill off Tuvalu's coral reefs through a process known as coral bleaching. Those reefs are essential for dampening the force of waves that lash Tuvalu's coasts and the fish that live alongside the coral are a vital source of food. Tuvalu is also likely to face more frequent and more violent weather conditions.

Already, existing coastal *pulaka* and coconut crops have been poisoned by the rising salt water. Some farmers have taken to growing *pulaka* in tin containers, but that's not a long-term solution. Tuvaluans say that many small *motus* (outer islets), such as Tepuka Savilivili Islet in Funafuti Lagoon, have lost all their coconut trees already, and without the trees to anchor what soil exists, those islets quickly become mere barren rocks. It's possible that this could simply be the result of a shorter-term shift in tidal conditions and currents, and it isn't the immediate future for all of Tuvalu. But an island becomes unable to sustain a permanent human population long before it is completely barren. There are no surplus crops in Tuvalu – it would not take much to push these islands over the edge.

Exactly what the future holds for Tuvalu depends on whether greenhouse-effect predictions are accurate, but even the most moderate predictions are dire. The Intergovernmental Panel on Climate Change, a United Nations body, lists Tuvalu as one of several Pacific countries that are likely to be rendered uninhabitable, even under conservative climate-change models, in the next 50–100 years. Atolls among the Cook Islands, Tokelau, French Polynesia, the Solomon Islands, and the Federated States of Micronesia will also be affected. People on some of those atolls have the option of relocating to larger islands of the same country – although even those larger islands will be under considerable pressure as they lose their coral reefs and fertile lowlands. But Tuvalu, Kiribati, Tokelau and the Marshall Islands are unique in being Pacific nations made up entirely of low-lying coral atolls and reef islands. For Tuvaluans, I-Kiribati, Tokelauans and Marshallese, there is nowhere to hide.

So what's Tuvalu doing about the greenhouse effect? It is doing what it can – minimising its own greenhouse gas emissions and protecting what resources it has through such initiatives as the Funafuti Conservation Area. But, as the government knows well, the contributions of tiny developing nations such as Tuvalu to the greenhouse effect is minuscule, and so too is the effect that they can have through direct methods. Instead, Tuvalu has forced itself onto the world stage, with statesmen such as Bikenibeu Paeniu and

the late Ionatana Ionatana speaking at international climate-change forums on the dangers Tuvalu faces.

Despite these measures, the government has been forced to face the grim likelihood that Tuvalu's atolls will become unviable. To pretend that the greenhouse effect might never happen is irresponsible of fossil-fuel company executives in Australia and the USA, but the Tuvaluan government simply cannot afford to bury its head in the sand. As a final contingency plan the Tuvalu government is lobbying New Zealand, Australia and Fiji for assurances that Tuvaluans can move to those countries if and when Tuvalu becomes uninhabitable. So far the government has met with limited success.

Even if an alternative overseas home is made available, forced relocation will have a terrible effect on Tuvaluans. Like all Polynesians they value their land above everything. In the Tuvaluan language, a person without land is known as *fakaalofa*, literally, a person deserving of pity. But in a hundred years, all Tuvaluans may well be *fakaalofa*.

'E ola matou iluga I fenua malalo kae foliki, te laukele se gata tena taaua. Te galo ifo o laukele ki lalo ite tai fanaka, se fakamaseiga te laa se toe mafai o suigina.'

'We live on small islands, and on small islands, land is priceless. Losing it as a result of rising sea levels would be a tragic, irreplaceable loss.'
(former prime minister Ionatana Ionatana in a speech to the United Nations)

Meleane Pese was the meteorological observer on Funafuti when Cyclone Bebe hit the atoll in October 1972. Her actions that night earned her a medal for bravery.

Bebe was Tuvalu's worst cyclone in living memory – it coincided with an unusually high spring tide, and three huge 'tidal' waves, driven by the cyclone, washed right over the low-lying atoll.

Meleane says that the elders can predict storms by the amount of fruit on the breadfruit trees. 'But we didn't notice that. It was only when I went to work and they gave me all the warnings that we knew the wind was coming. But we didn't know about the tidal wave, we had no warning.' She describes the first wave: 'We were all in the observatory building. The wave went through the Telecom building next door; it didn't affect us in the observatory much. The second tidal wave broke the windows and took the roof off the observatory. Only the bricks stayed.'

When the third wave hit, the staff of the office were swept out of the building. Meleane saved the lives of a woman and her child by holding them to her as she clung to a tree. 'I looked for something to hold on and I got hold of a coconut tree that was the biggest. I lost my watch. I remember looking at 2.10 pm and next my watch was gone – washed off my wrist. I found my watch under that coconut tree the next day when I went back. I was very frightened that night.'

'The second tidal wave broke the windows and took the roof off the observatory. Only the bricks stayed.'

Funafuti Atoll was devastated, swept clean by the cyclone. Few houses, or even coconut trees, were left standing when people emerged from the shelter of the two pastors' houses the next day. Instead, a rampart of coral rubble had been thrown up around the ocean side of the atoll's islets. It is now the main topographical feature of the atoll, and includes its highest points.

Almost 800 people were left homeless by Cyclone Bebe. Miraculously, only five people were killed. Ironically, one of them was a meteorological technician stationed at the observatory.

'We drank the milk from coconuts until, after a week, relief came from Tarawa, Kiribati,' says Meleane. Cyclone Bebe is commemorated with Hurricane Day on 21 October every year with a holiday on Funafuti.

The late prime minister of Tuvalu, the Honourable Ionatana Ionatana, was a driving force behind the publication of this book. Sadly, he died suddenly in early 2001, before the project was completed.

Ionatana was born and raised on Funafuti Atoll, Tuvalu's capital. He started his career in 1956 as a policeman back in the British colonial days of the Gilbert & Ellice Islands and rose to become second-in-command of the colony's police force, and later chief of police in 1976 when Tuvalu was separated from the colony. In 1977, a year before independence, Ionatana transferred to the civil service and was made secretary to government. A natural politician, Ionatana entered the Tuvaluan parliament in 1985 and in 1999 he became prime minister.

As prime minister, one of Ionatana's greatest public relations coups was to successfully close The .tv Corporation Internet licensing deal. Ionatana oversaw a time of unprecedented economic strength for Tuvalu. Underpinned by national savings, fisheries and The .tv Corporation income, Tuvalu invested in local infrastructure, health, education and transport. The country became a full member of the Commonwealth (the new name for the old British Commonwealth) and the United Nations.

Ionatana was Tuvalu's spokesman on climate change and the greenhouse effect, speaking around the world on the risks that small Pacific countries face unless the world acts to reduce greenhouse gas emissions. Ionatana's hope was that this book, a showpiece

'Tuvaluans are seeking a place they can permanently migrate to, should the high tides eventually make our homes uninhabitable.'

of Tuvaluan culture, would help persuade the world that that culture is worth saving from the rising seas and worsening storms that climate change will bring. He brought the plight of Tuvalu to the world stage and asked other nations to look to the future: 'Tuvaluans are seeking a place they can permanently migrate to, should the high tides eventually make our homes uninhabitable.'

When Ionatana suddenly died, after being struck by a heart attack while speaking at a function in Funafuti, Tuvalu, and the world, mourned. He was a pioneer, a motivator and a natural leader

end note

The concentration of carbon dioxide (CO_2) and other greenhouse gases in the atmosphere is growing. The threat of atmospheric warming is here to stay. No industrial country has shown any real will to curb greenhouse gas emissions. The Climate Change Conference is presently on hold. The Kyoto Protocol is teetering on the brink of failure. The United Nations' Intergovernmental Panel on Climate Change has sounded the alarm – is sounding the alarm – but to what extent is it being heard?

Six billion people around the world rely on carbon-based fuel for energy to warm (and cool) their houses, heat their stoves, light their workplaces, drive steam turbines, and to power the ubiquitous internal combustion engine.

Scientists first voiced the possibility of man-made global warming in the early 1970s. In 2001, the estimated sea level rise in the southwest Pacific is 2mm per year. In the next 50–100 years Tuvalu is likely to be rendered uninhabitable. It's not just that the sea level will rise and Tuvalu will be submerged – the rising saltwater table below will poison deep-rooted plants; the higher temperatures of the sea will kill coral reefs; and the fish that live in the reefs will lose their environment.

Nanumea

N

Niutao

Nanumaga

Nui

Vaitupu

Nukufetau

Funafuti

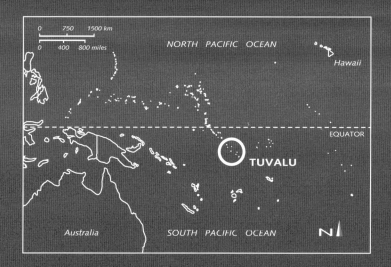

0   750   1500 km

0   400   800 miles

NORTH   PACIFIC   OCEAN

Hawaii

EQUATOR

○ **TUVALU**

Australia   SOUTH   PACIFIC   OCEAN   N

Nukulaelae

0   50   100 km

0   30   60 miles

Niulakita

image index

Vaitupu Island, May 2000. *Talofa* (hello or welcome) sign for the Constitutional Review Committee's (CRC) visit. Vaitupu's church is in the background.

Funafuti Atoll, July 1999. Across the lagoon from the capital, Fualopa is an uninhabited islet in Funafuti Conservation Area. The area is a great success. People visit the islet to picnic.

Nui Atoll, May 2000. Unloading pigpen materials from the *Nivanga II*'s workboat. A project to contain the island's pigs was initiated by Nui's island council to restore the islet's interior.

Funafuti Atoll, December 2000. Full moon over the lagoon. View across the lagoon to the conservation area. Just visible on the horizon are the atoll's eastern islets.

Funafuti Atoll, July 1999. Nukufetau's Island Day celebrations. Children rest in the Nukufetau *falekaupule*. Tuvalu's island communities have their own *falekaupules* on Funafuti. The *falekaupules* are focal points for these communities.

Funafuti Atoll, December 2000. Tepuka Islet. This islet was used by the US in WWII as a radio and operations centre.

Funafuti Atoll, July 1999. Ice cream is an import eagerly awaited, especially by children.

Funafuti Atoll, July 1999. Late in the day Funafutians head for the lagoon. Next to the Vaiaku Lagi Hotel this group of children hold an impromptu swimming carnival.

Funafuti Atoll, February 2000. Exposure by the light of the full moon. This full moon coincides with the southern hemisphere's lunar perigee of 364,494kms. Only every 133 years does the moon come this close to the earth.

Funafuti Atoll, December 2000. Adjacent to the Funafuti Community Falekaupule, children prepare to snorkel in the lagoon. Funafuti suffers from a burgeoning population, due in part to migration from the outer islands.

Vaitupu Island, May 2000. Vaitupu's current town wharf is the second wharf constructed as part of a Japanese aid project. The first was finished and subsequently washed away by a storm.

Funafuti Atoll, February 2000. Grandmother and grandchildren in a modern house, ocean-side. While hotter than the open-sided traditional dwellings these houses are popular for their tin roofs, used to collect rainwater

Vaitupu Island, June 1998. Vaitupu viewed from the sea at sunrise while fishing for bonito. From the sea the low-lying islands are easily lost from sight, particularly if bad weather sets in. It is not uncommon for fisherman to be lost at sea.

Funafuti Atoll, February 2000. Children playing soccer in a flooded area during spring tides. The 3.2m high tides sparked the world's concern as they threatened to inundate the country.

Niutao Atoll, February 2001. A young girl looks out to sea.

Nanumea Atoll, February 2001. The WWII wreckage of a four-engined B24 Liberator bomber recycled for use as coconut storage.

Funafuti Atoll, July 1999. The US Navy 'Seabees' Construction Battalion built Funafuti's airfield in 1942. The airfield occupies the largest part of the capital islet's land area.

Nanumea Atoll, February 2001. Lakena Islet. The graves of Tuvaluans are decorated with WWII-vintage Coca-Cola bottles. Lakena is permanently populated by two families; they're joined most days by Nanumeans from the main populated islet who tend gardens on the islet.

Funafuti Atoll, December 2000. Prime Minister Ionatana Ionatana addresses parliament in the *falekaupule* next to the airstrip. The sitting was later disrupted by an incoming flight.

Funafuti Atoll, December 2000. Vaiaku Lagi Hotel. Twenty-minute exposure taken by the light of the full moon from a 2nd-floor room in the hotel.

Nukufetau Atoll, May 2000. Primary school, lagoonside. Tuvalu sees that its future lies in the education of its young people.

Nukulaelae Atoll, December 2000. Kelese Simona is 88; he lives, like most Tuvaluans, with his extended family. It's usual to find three generations living under the one roof. *Palagis* are the only people to live alone in Tuvalu.

Funafuti Atoll, April 2000. Elia Tavita, *kaupule* president. Bomb Day commemoration, Tausoa Lima Falekaupule.

Vaitupu Island, May 2000. Watching the sun go down from Vaitupu's town wharf. On Kioa, a Fijian island settled by Tuvaluans from Vaitupu, the village is divided into sunset and sunrise communities.

Nukulaelae Atoll, December 2000. Headed for the Elekana Monument across Nukulaelae's lagoon.

Vaitupu Island, May 2000. *Fatele* for the members of the CRC in the island's *falekaupule*. The CRC, comprising government delegates, toured the islands canvassing local opinion on changes to Tuvalu's constitution.

Nukufetau Atoll, May 2000. Lagoon-side, watching sunrise as Tuvalu's cargo and passenger ship the *Nivaga II* rests at anchor. The *Nivaga II* also serves as a training vessel for the Tuvalu Maritime Training Institute.

Nukulaelae Atoll, December 2000. Malaki Mauga, *ulu aliki* (chief), carving a canoe for *pule o kaupule* (president) Aifou Tafie. Malaki has been working the breadfruit tree log for two weeks.

Nui Atoll, May 2000. Nui's elders dance in a *fatele* for members of the CRC.

Vaitupu Island, May 2000. *Fatele* for the CRC in Vaitupu's *falekaupule*. No effort was spared by the island communities in preparing for the CRC's visits.

Nanumaga Atoll, February 2001. Weaving a *tapola* (basket) out of coconut fronds.

Nukufetau Atoll, May 2000. Women dance on pandanus mats. *Fatele* involves harmonious singing to an ever-increasing drumbeat.

Nukulaelae Atoll, December 2000. Malaki Mauga sailing his canoe. With a sail made from rice bags and a sheet, and a halyard salvaged from washed-up ropes, the outrigger is surprisingly quick and fun.

Funafuti Atoll, April 2000. Pateni Vakalasi and Linosia Unitelo's wedding. After a few words from Linosia's father the newlyweds depart for the reception in a van decorated with balloons and snack foods.

Funafuti Atoll, April 2000. The reception for Pateni and Linosia's wedding is held in the *falekaupule*. An open invitation was made to the hotel's guests. As is the custom Pateni and Linosia endured many changes of clothes.

Nukufetau Atoll, February 2001. Siona Fou Church.

Nukufetau Atoll, May 2000. Children at the Siona Fou Church entrance.

Niutao Atoll, February 2001. Niutao's church.

Niulakita Atoll, December 2000. Church interior. Niulakita's church bell was acquired from a ship and turned out to be too heavy to lift into the tiny tower, so it's housed in a nearby shelter.

Niutao Atoll, February 2001. Seona Paneva, martial arts expert, with the spear his ancestor used to kill the *palagi* (Europeans) caught bathing in the island's well. Water is still a precious commodity in Tuvalu.

Niutao Atoll, February 2001. A traditional house. Beams made of lightweight pandanus trunks are tied together and support beautifully thatched roofs. Germinating nuts and a bird-catching net are stored on the beams and rafters.

Nanumaga Atoll, February 2001. Atoa Kelemeni sits at the entrance to his traditional house. More and more of the new houses on the islands are 'palagi (European-style) houses': dull concrete-blocks roofed with corrugated iron.

Nui Atoll, May 2000. Everybody lends a hand to unload bags of rice and other supplies from *Nivaga II*'s workboats.

Kioa Island, Fiji, January 2001. Kaisame Kirisome was born on Vaitupu. In 1946 fearing overcrowding the people of Vaitupu bought Kioa in Fiji, and Kaisame migrated. Kioa has a Tuvaluan society, but Kaisame wants to return to Vaitupu to die.

Vaitupu Island, May 2000. Tepoutoa Epati, birdcaller, with his wife and grandchild at the entrance to their house.

Funafuti Atoll, December 2000. Children at the airport terminal. Watching to see who is arriving by plane is a favourite pastime in Funafuti.

Nukufetau Atoll, February 2001. Interior of a modern house. With no TV broadcast to the outer islands, videos are popular. On Nukufetau everyone's favourite video was *Braveheart*.

Funafuti Atoll, December 2000. Asiva Motorcycle Hire. Funafuti's potholed roads are tough on vehicles and keep speeds down to a fast walk. A new road system for Funafuti will be completed by the end of 2001.

Nukulaelae Atoll, December 2000. Tubwebwe Teoli. Tubwebwe, from Kiribati, married a Tuvaluan and moved to Nukulaelae. Expert in herbal medicine, she crushes *nonu* fruit for a traditional remedy.

Funafuti Atoll, December 2000. Traffic control: Tuvalu's only stop sign.

Funafuti Atoll, July 1999. Mother and son, Princess Margaret Hospital. The hospital was opened in 1978 as part of Princess Margaret's royal visit as the official British presence when Tuvalu became independent.

Nui Atoll, May 2000. On the left is senior staff nurse Terube Alinesi. 'In my family I have to do the cooking and look after the family and here at the hospital I have to look after the patients.'

Nanumea Atoll, February 2001. Akoakoga Kalala, one of the few policewomen in Tuvalu, aboard the catamaran for Lakena Islet.

Funafuti Atoll, December 2000. Cadets from the Tuvalu Maritime Training Institute on Amatuku Islet help unload a workboat.

Funafuti Atoll, May 2000. Tuvalu Maritime Training Institute passing out parade. These cadets have undertaken a rigorous education, graduating as motormen, deckhands and cooks. All graduates will be offered places on merchant ships.

Niutao Atoll, February 2001. A large part of the school curriculum is dedicated to learning English, and stories pinned up on the wall of a classroom at the Uepele Primary School tell tales of everyday island life.

Niutao Atoll, February 2001. Primary school children.

Funafuti Atoll, July 1999. Students work with a cargo handling simulator provided under an Australian aid program, Tuvalu Maritime Training Institute.

Vaitupu Island, June 1998. Toaripi House, Motufoua Secondary School Sports Day. The *Nivaga II* collects relatives of the students from all of Tuvalu's islands and takes them home again at the end of the two-day event.

Nukufetau Atoll, February 2001. Tutasi Memorial School Day celebrates the opening of the school in 1947. The first primary school in Tuvalu, it was established and run at the local community's initiative and expense.

P&O Nedlloyd Fos, July 2000. Part of the Tuvaluan crew of a German cargo ship, Manase Niusila and Ligitase Taue take a coffee break as their ship makes its way through Bass Strait, Australia.

P&O Nedlloyd Fos, July 2000. Haumili Haleti, AB, keeps watch over stevedoring operations at West Swanson Dock, Melbourne, Australia.

Nui Atoll, May 2000. Passengers head ashore in the workboat from *Nivaga II*, Tuvalu's cargo and passenger ship.

Vaitapu Island, May 2000. On *Nivaga II*, seamen prepare to unload cargo before sunrise.

Vaitupu Island, May 2000. Passengers disembark *Nivaga II*.

Nui Atoll, May 2000. Islanders arrive in the workboat for departure to Nukufetau aboard *Nivaga II*.

Vaitupu Island, June 1998. Parents disembark the *Nivaga II* for the Motufoua Secondary School Sports Day.

Vaitupu Island, February 2001. Tuvalu's fishing boat, the *Manaui*, and its captain. As well as fishing the *Manaui* often carries passengers and general cargo.

Vaitupu Island, June 1998. Fishing for bonito. A project is being undertaken to provide all fishermen with a compass and flares. It's hoped that one day radios and GPS receivers will be standard equipment.

Funafuti Atoll, July 1999. Canoe at sunset in Funafuti Lagoon.

Funafuti Atoll, December 2000. Children play near the hotel.

Funafuti Atoll, July 1999. Boys with a captive turtle in a borrow pit. During WWII more than 400,000 cubic metres of coral was excavated (borrowed) to level the airfield.

Kioa, Fiji, January 2001. Tuvaluans playing *kilikiti*, a Polynesian version of cricket.

Funafuti Atoll, July 1999. Nukufetau islanders playing *ano* on the airfield. *Ano* is a uniquely Tuvaluan game, the ball is a rock encased in pandanus leaves.

Funafuti Atoll, July 1999. Soccer training at night on the runway.

Niulakita Atoll, December 2000. Cards at the pastor's house. Social activities take place here as Niulakita has no *falekaupule*. The *falekaupule* and most of the village were destroyed by a cyclone.

Nanumaga Atoll, February 2001. Women from the Mouhala clan put on an impromptu performance.

Funafuti Atoll, December 2000. Children at play.

Funafuti Atoll, July 1999. Children swimming in Funafuti Lagoon.

Nukufetau Atoll, February 2001. Children play in the rain.

Nukufetau Atoll, February 2001. Sliding down the boat ramp.

Nanumea Atoll, February 2001. Boys playing on the ocean side of the island.

Nukufetau Atoll, February 2001. Choir practice in a traditional sleeping house.

Funafuti Atoll, February 2000. A tuna is carried down the atoll's main street.

Niutao Atoll, February 2001. Motorcycles are the main form of transport in Tuvaluan villages.

Nui Atoll, May 2000. Fenua Tapu islet. Aloloima Sipane peels taro for feasting in the *falekaupule*.

Nui Atoll, May 2000. Nui's elders hold an impromptu meeting in the town centre.

Vaitupu Island, May 2000. Maaia Moupa harvests toddy from a dwarf coconut palm. Originating in Sri Lanka, dwarf palms save Tuvaluans from the twice-a-day 20m climb it would take to shimmy a regular coconut palm.

Nui Atoll, May 2000. Traditional housing. Open-sided to let the breeze flow through, these houses are cool despite the oppressive tropical heat and humidity.

Nukulaelae Atoll, December 2000. *Pulaka*, a root vegetable, is mixed with toddy.

Vaitupu Island, May 2000. Tepoutoa Epati, 63 years old, preparing to call *taketake* birds from his *puka* tree. The tree is about 30m high.

Funafuti Atoll, July 1999. Tuvaluan women in the kitchen with an outboard engine.

Funafuti Atoll, December 2000. Sleeping platform by the airstrip.

Kioa, Fiji, January 2001. Trade store, stocked with the ubiquitous tinned corn beef. This store is well stocked compared with many on Tuvalu's outer islands.

Nukulaelae Atoll, December 2000. Taking a break in the shade of a coconut palm near the Elekana monument.

Funafuti Atoll, April 2000. Roasted pig decorated with cigarettes and chewing gum is served at Pateni Vakalasi and Linosia Unitelo's wedding.

Funafuti Atoll, December 2000. Crabs, pawpaw, bananas and breadfruit. Island food prepared for a communal meal at the pastor's house.

Nukufetau Atoll, May 2000. This family have moved into one of two wards at the medical centre. They're enjoying a meal of coconut crab. Nukufetau is renown for its abundant coconut crabs.

Nukufetau Atoll, May 2000. Temotuloto Islet. Fish drying in the sun.

Nui Atoll, May 2000. Apalosa Limon cooking a pig for feasting at the *falekaupule*.

Nukufetau Atoll, May 2000. Propelled by rubber bands, the boys' spears are made from concrete reinforcing rods. These small fish will supplement a pig's diet of coconut.

Nukufetau Atoll, May 2000. Coconut crabs at a *falekaupule* feast. Coconut crabs are a much prized food source, often appearing for special occasions. They can be 40 years old by the time they reach their maximum size of about 4kg.

Niulakita Atoll, December 2000. Lunch for the community is held at the pastor's house. Most of Niulakita's 39 residents were present at the lunch.

Funafuti Atoll, December 2000. Family fishing on Funafala Islet. The girl is biting the fish's head to kill it.

Nukufetau Atoll, February 2001. Fish in an outrigger canoe. This outrigger, propelled by a small, four-horsepower outboard, is fast enough to troll from.

Nanumea Atoll, February 2001. Flying fishing. *Palagi* lights lure the fish to the surface and illuminate them. A moonless night is required to give the light maximum effect.

Nanumea Atoll, February 2001. Fish fly in all directions. It is not uncommon to be hit in the head by a fish missile.

Nanumea Atoll, February 2001. Flying fish simply fly into the boats.

Nanumea Atoll, February 2001. The fisherman skilfully catches a fish as it leaps from the water.

Nanumea Atoll, February 2001. Fish are caught below the surface as well as in midair.

Funafuti Atoll, December 2000. Laki Kalapu drifted away from shore twice: once he landed in Pago Pago in American Samoa, once in Futuna (the second island of the French colony of Wallis & Futuna).

Funafuti Atoll, July 1999. Land for housing is limited on Funafuti. This family from an outer island have built their house next to a borrow pit.

Funafuti Atoll, December 2000. The tiny islet of Tepuka Savilivili has been cited as possible evidence of climatic change, as its coconut trees and sandbanks have disappeared leaving it just a small stretch of rock.

Funafuti Atoll, February 2000. Spring tides flood Funafuti's borrow pits. The pits are used as rubbish dumps and pigsties, and are an unhealthy eyesore.

Funafuti Atoll, July 1999. Frigates and terns fly above Fualopa, one of several uninhabited islets set aside for conservation.

Nui Atoll, May 2000. Remains of a US B24 Liberator that survived a forced landing in the lagoon intact. All 11 crew survived. It was subsequently blown up by the US to mislead any Japanese reconnaissance of the atoll.

Funafuti Atoll, December 2000. Tepuka Islet is an uninhabited islet north of the Funafuti Conservation Area. Landowners visit regularly to fish, harvest coconuts and catch birds.

Funafuti Atoll, July 1999. A shortage of land on Funafuti has led to housing being built around and on the rubbish-filled borrow pits, from which coral was excavated to build the airfield.

Funafuti Atoll, December 2000. Fualopa Islet, part of the Funafuti Conservation Area, which is 33 sq km of protected lagoon, reef, channels, ocean and islets. The zone was established in 1999.

Funafuti Atoll, December 2000. People often sleep on the runway to avoid overcrowded and hot modern houses.

Funafuti Atoll, April 2000. Meleane Pese was the meteorological observer at the time of Cyclone Bebe, in 1972. She saved the lives of a woman and her child by holding them to a coconut tree as a tidal wave washed over.

Funafuti Atoll, July 1999. The late Honourable Ionatana Ionatana, former prime minister of Tuvalu, and his son.

Funafuti Atoll, February 2000. View east over Funafuti's lagoon at night.

glossary

akiaki – Tuvaluan term for white tern, a kind of sea bird

aliki – chief

ano – traditional ball game

atoll – low-lying island built up from successive deposits of coral, typically irregular in shape, enclosing a shallow lagoon

blackbirders – ships which carried away large numbers of Pacific islanders during the mid-19th century to work as slaves mining the phosphate deposits of islands off the South American coast, north Queensland and elsewhere

borrow pits – ten huge pits left from the construction of Funafuti's airfield during World War II, when the US construction corps excavated or 'borrowed' over 400,000 cubic metres of coral. The pits are now a difficult environmental problem, filled with rubbish and regularly flooded.

coconut crab – huge, edible land crab related to the hermit crab, so-called because of its ability to open coconuts with its formidable nippers. As coconut crabs are slow to mature, conservation measures are encouraged to ensure their survival and proliferation.

fatele – traditional music and dance performance; the word means 'to multiply' and indicates the steadily increasing tempo throughout the *fatele*

fakaalofa – landless person

falekaupule – traditional village meeting hall; every atoll has at least one and on Funafuti there is a *falekaupule* for each of the islands in the group, for use by local residents who are from those other islands. The term *maneapa*, a Kiribati word, is sometimes used.

feitu – village side: Tuvaluan villages or whole islands are often divided into two sides, originally a geographic split, but people retain membership of their *feitu* even when they relocate elsewhere. Many aspects of village life from *fatele* dances to building projects involve the community working as two competing sides.

fenua – land, or the people who live on that land

fou – flowered head wreaths worn on festivals, feasts and *fatele*. A *fou* can have mysterious powers and Tuvaluans are wary of accepting a *fou* from a stranger since it could put a spell on them.

fusi – cooperative store

I-Kiribati – the people of the Kiribati islands

kaupule – elected island council; the local government led by a president and secretary

katipopuki – hardwood spear

kilikiti – a Polynesian version of cricket

lagoon – a body of water bounded by a raised encircling reef

Micronesia – Greek for 'small islands'; the scattered small islands of the north-west Pacific including the Federated States of Micronesia, the Marianas, Palau, the Marshall Islands and Kiribati

motu – island or islet at an atoll's perimeter

nonu – fruit with medicinal properties, recently a modest craze in the West

noddy – a tropical tern, or aquatic bird, with black and white or dark plumage

palagi – European or Westerner

Polynesia – Greek for 'many islands'; the scattered islands of the south-central Pacific including the Cook Islands, French Polynesia, Samoa, Tonga, Tokelau and Tuvalu. The so-called Polynesian Triangle stretches from New Zealand and Hawaii to French Polynesia.

pulaka – a taro-like plant which is a principal part of the island diet, grown in *pulaka* pits, which are excavated over many generations and filled with composted soil

panakua – literally 'seven virgins'; a stone or wood carving which when set outside on the order of the *aliki* is thought to bring rain

pandanus – a common tree whose sword-shaped leaves are used to make mats and baskets. It produces fruit which can be eaten and is used in traditional medicine.

puka – large-foliaged tropical softwood tree used for building local canoes

pule o kaupule – president of the island council

taketake – Tuvaluan term for black noddy, a kind of sea bird

taro – a plant with green heart-shaped leaves, cultivated for both its leaf and edible rootstock; the latter is commonly boiled and eaten like a potato

te sina o fenua – island council of elders; literally, the island's 'grey-hairs'

toddy – coconut tree sap tapped from the spathe (unopened flower). Fresh toddy has a light vaguely lemonade-ish taste and can be used in cooking; fermented it becomes alcoholic sour toddy or can be boiled to make molasses.

tofuga – priests of the pre-Christian religion of Tuvalu

ulu aliki – head chief

Note: some terms differ from island to island

further reading

Becke, Louis. *South Seas Supercargo: Stories by Louis Becke.* Honolulu: University of Hawaii Press, 1967.

Besnier, Niko. *Ttou Tauloto te Ggana Tuuvalu – A Course in the Tuvaluan Language.* Funafuti: US Peace Corps, 1981.

Besnier, Niko. *Tuvalu Lexicon.* Funafuti: US Peace Corps, 1981.

Besnier, Niko. *Literacy, Emotion and Authority: Reading and Writing on a Polynesian Atoll (Nukulaelae).* Cambridge: Cambridge University Press, 1995.

Chambers, Keith, and Anne Chambers. *Unity of Heart: Culture and Change in a Polynesian Atoll Society.* Prospect Heights, IL: Waveland Press Inc, 2001.

Chambers, Keith. *Heirs of Tefolaha – Tradition & Social Organization in Nanumea, A Polynesian Atoll Community.* PhD thesis. 1984.

Coates, Austin. *Western Pacific Islands.* London: Her Majesty's Stationary Office, 1970.

David, Mrs Edgeworth. *Funafuti, or Three Months on a Coral Atoll: An Unscientific Account of a Scientific Expedition.* London: John Murray, 1899.

Ells, Philip. *The People's Lawyer.* London: Virgin Publications, 2000.

Grimble, Arthur. *A Pattern of Islands.* London: Penguin, 1952.

Grimble, Arthur. *Return to the Islands: Life and Legend in the Gilberts.* New York: William Morrow, 1957.

Hedley, Charles. *General Account of the Atoll Funafuti.* Australian Museum Memoir 3 (part 1, pp. 1–71). 1896.

Jackson, Geoffrey W. *Te Tikisionale o te 'Gana Tuvalu: A Tuvaluan-English Dictionary.* Suva: Oceania Printers, 1994.

Jackson, Geoffrey, and Jenny Jackson. *An Introduction to Tuvaluan.* Suva: Oceania Printers, 1999.

Kennedy, Donald Gilbert. *Field Notes on the Culture of Vaitupu – Ellice Islands (Memoirs of the Polynesian Society).* New Zealand: New Plymouth, 1931.

Koch, Gerd. *The Material Culture of Tuvalu.* University of the South Pacific, Institute of Pacific Studies, 1961 (translated 1984).

Koch, Klaus-Friedrich. *Logs in the Current of the Sea.* Canberra: Australian National University Press, 1978.

Laracy, Hugh (ed). *Tuvalu: A History.* Suva: University of the South Pacific, Institute of Pacific Studies, 1983.

Macdonald, Barrie. *Cinderellas of the Empire: Towards a History of Kiribati and Tuvalu.* Canberra: Australian National University Press, 1982.

Maude, H.E. *Of Islands and Men: Studies in Pacific History.* Melbourne: Oxford University Press, 1968.

McQuarrie, Peter. *Strategic Atolls: Tuvalu and the Second World War.* Suva: University of the South Pacific, Institute of Pacific Studies, 1994.

Munro, Doug. *The Lagoon Islands: a History of Tuvalu 1820–1908.* Australia: Macquarie University, School of History, Philosophy and Politics, 1982.

thanks

Many thanks go to the people of Tuvalu for their great hospitality and assistance during this project. In particular, thanks to the late prime minister Ionatana Ionatana, and to Saufatu Sopoanga, Panapasi Nelesone, Amasone Kilei, Koloa Telake, Sam Telake, Pokia Tihala, Bikenibeu Paeniu, Brendan McHarg, Hilia Vavae, Tataua Pese, Opetia Simati, Ken Bartlett and Tito Tapugao and the Tuvalu Maritime Training Institute. Thanks also to the South Pacific Agency, the Vaiaku Lagi Hotel and the captain and crew of the MV *Manaui*. Thanks to Volker Ueckert of F. Laeisz Line, operator of the MV *P&O Nedlloyd Fos*.

On Funafuti thanks to John Hensford and Eti Esela of Alpha Shipping, and Dr Uschi Kaly, James Conway, Sharon Marks and Paul Scells. On Niulakita thanks to Alafaio Honolulu (the pastor), Pelusia Tauetia (the radio operator), Elifaleti Sosene (the meteorological officer), Tealikisele Talapai (the island chief), Muaifomo Kusi (the temporary nurse) and everybody else on the island who entertained us, showed us around and put on a huge meal with very limited warning. On Nukufetau thanks to Peneueta George. On Nukulaelae thanks to Leata Lomi and Iolita Mautinoa who showed us all around their beautiful island; Eunike Tonise and Siata Halama who joined us later in the day to feed us lunch, take us to other islets in the lagoon and show us how to catch coconut crabs; Selau Toematagi who drove the boat; Aifou Tafie (the island *pule o kaupule*); and to expert canoe carver Malaki Mauga. On Nanumea thanks to Akoakoga Kalala (the police officer), Fiafiaga Katalake (the nurse) and Naomi Nukunonu (the pastor's wife). Thanks to Vaguna Satupa (the *pule o kaupule*) and Seono Paneva on Niutao. On Vaitupu thanks to Namoliki Sualiki (the Motufoua school headmaster), Frank Mars and Emma Smallacombe (VSO volunteer teachers), Tui Taumafai, Tepoutoa Epati, and Ron Vetter. On Nanumaga thanks to Sefuteni Liki (the *pule o kaupule*), Paka Simona (the *fusi* manager), Tanei Taumafai, Tofiga Falani, Naumati Lameko and the other women of the mat-making co-op. On Nui thanks to Leitonga Taua; and on Kioa thanks to Alfred Kaisame.

In the USA thanks to Paul Alapati, Ted Hong and Lou Kerner of The .tv Corporation. In Australia thanks to Helen Sinclair, Susan Olle and Jo Daniell. In Fiji thanks to Angenette Heffernan; and in Samoa thanks to Jan Sinclair.

Thanks to Floris de Bonneville and Rowena Hockin.

Special thanks to the Tuvaluan government for use of the fisheries patrol boat HTMSS *Te Mataili* (left), and to Commanding Officers Mika Elisaia and Talafou Esekia and crew.

Time & Tide: The Islands of Tuvalu

1st edition – 2001

Published by
Lonely Planet Publications Pty Ltd
ABN 36 005 607 983
90 Maribyrnong St, Footscray,
Victoria 3011, Australia

Lonely Planet Offices
Australia Locked Bag 1, Footscray, Victoria 3011
USA 150 Linden Street, Oakland, CA 94607
UK 10a Spring Place, London NW5 3BH
France 1 rue du Dahomey, 75011, Paris

Printed by The Bookmaker International Ltd
Printed in China

Photographs
The images in this book are available for licensing from Lonely Planet Images.
email: lpi@lonelyplanet.com.au

ISBN 1 86450 342 4

text & map © Lonely Planet Publications Pty Ltd 2001
photographs © Peter Bennetts 2001

Designer: Karen Nettelfield
Editor: Bridget Blair
Senior Editor: Martine Lleonart
Editorial Consultants: Errol Hunt & James Conway

Thanks to: Martin Heng, David Kemp, Jane Pennells, Peter Cruttenden and Elisa Coffman